© 2002 by Barbour Publishing, Inc.

1-58660-796-0

Cover image © PhotoDisc

Interior illustrations by Todd Smith.

Published by Barbour Books, an imprint of Barbour Publishing, Inc., P.O. Box 719, Uhrichsville, Ohio 44683, www.barbourbooks.com

Member of the
Evangelical Christian
Publishers Association

Printed in China.
5 4 3 2

World's Best Mommy

KELLY KOHL

DayMaker
GREETING BOOKS

Mother's Love

Her love is like an island
In life's ocean, vast and wide,
A peaceful, quiet shelter
From the wind, the rain, the tide.
'Tis bound on the North by Hope,
By Patience on the West,
By tender Counsel on the South
And on the East by Rest.
Above it like a beacon light
Shine Faith, and Truth, and Prayer;
And thro' the changing scenes of life
I find a haven there.

AUTHOR UNKNOWN

Introduction

You are receiving this little book because, from a "little" perspective that means "a lot," you are the world's best mommy. Out of all the mothers in the world, you were hand-picked by God to love and care for your child. . .and to guide him or her into adulthood.

Enjoy the quotations, stories, prayers, and poetry throughout—all of which will remind you of the special role you play in your child's life. And cherish the unique fill-in and coloring pages your child has completed especially for you. This is a treasured keepsake in honor of you—the world's best mommy!

Mother's Love

Mother's love is peace.
It need not be acquired; it need not be deserved.
ERICH FROMM

A mother understands
what a child does not say.
JEWISH PROVERB

The Beauty of a Mother's Love

Jared didn't want to share with his sister, Olivia. He knew he was disobeying his mother, but he really didn't want his sister playing with his blue balloon. So he jerked the balloon out of her hands and cried, "No!" His mother gently, but firmly, explained that his sister deserved a turn playing with the balloon. . .and Jared had to accept it. He apologized to his mom and found another toy to occupy his attention. Although he had disobeyed his mother, her love for him didn't waver. She forgave him in a matter of minutes and put his disobedience out of her mind.

A mother's love is like God's love for His children. She holds her children dear to her heart, and her love is unconditional. When her child does wrong, she is faithful in teaching him right. She forgives and holds no grudges—like our Lord forgives us for our sins, allowing us to move on and grow in His love.

Dear Lord,

Thank You for allowing me to experience the precious gift of motherhood and for giving me the opportunity to raise a child in this world. Please allow me to reflect Your love so my child can see You in me. Help me to show my child what it means to obey You and to receive You into his life.

Amen.

Being a good mommy is. . .

_____

_____

_____

_____

_____

_____

_____

_____

A Mother's Love

There are times when only a mother's love
Can understand our tears,
Can soothe our disappointments
And calm all of our fears.
There are times when only a mother's love
Can share the joy we feel
When something we've dreamed about
Quite suddenly is real.

There are times when only a mother's faith
Can help us on life's way
And inspire in us the confidence
We need from day to day.
For a mother's heart and a mother's faith
And a mother's steadfast love
Were fashioned by the angels
And sent from God above.

AUTHOR UNKNOWN

Mother love is the fuel that enables
a normal human being to do the impossible.

AUTHOR UNKNOWN

Her children arise
and call her blessed.

PROVERBS 31:28

The heart of a mother is a deep abyss at the bottom
of which you will always find forgiveness.

HONORE DE BALZAC

I love you, Mommy, because. . .

_____

_____

_____

_____

_____

_____

_____

_____

Who takes the child by the hand
takes the mother by the heart.
GERMAN PROVERB

A mother's arms are made
of tenderness, and
children sleep soundly in them.
VICTOR HUGO

I remember my mother's prayers,
and they have always followed me.
They have clung to me all my life.
ABRAHAM LINCOLN

Your love helps me grow, Mommy.

A picture memory brings to me;
I look across the years and see
Myself beside my mother's knee.
I feel her gentle hand restrain
My selfish moods, and know again
A child's blind sense of wrong and pain.
But wiser now, a man gray grown,
My childhood's needs are better known.
My mother's chastening love I own.

JOHN GREENLEAF WHITTIER

The History of Mother's Day

Mother's Day, the second Sunday in May, was first observed in 1908. It is believed to have originated when Anna Jarvis (1864–1948), of Philadelphia, Pennsylvania, began a campaign to establish it as a national holiday. She persuaded the congregation of her mother's church, Andrews Methodist Church, in Grafton, West Virginia, to celebrate Mother's Day on the second anniversary of her mother's death. Anna was extremely close to her mother and hoped that this holiday would help to increase children's appreciation of their mothers while they were still living. A few years later, President Woodrow Wilson officially declared the second Sunday in May as Mother's Day. This day is now observed in several countries around the world—including Mexico, Sweden, England, France, Denmark, China, and India.

Anna Jarvis on the purpose of Mother's Day...

...to revive the dormant filial love and gratitude we owe to those who gave us birth. To be a home tie for the absent. To obliterate family estrangement. To create a bond of brotherhood through the wearing of a floral badge. To make us better children by getting us closer to the hearts of our good mothers. To brighten the lives of good mothers. To have them know we appreciate them, though we do not show it as often as we ought....

Mother's Day is to remind us of our duty before it is too late. This day is intended that we may make new resolutions for a more active thought to our dear mothers. By words, gifts, acts of affection, and in every way possible, give her pleasure, and make her heart glad every day, and constantly keep in memory of Mother's Day; when you made this resolution, lest you forget and neglect your dear mother, if absent from home write her often, tell her of a few of her noble good qualities and how you love her.

A Mother's Day Corsage

Carnations have been linked to Mother's Day since the first observance in 1908, when Anna Jarvis supplied them at Andrews Methodist Church in honor of her mother. These flowers were her mother's favorite. The chosen color was white, representing a mother's pure and enduring love. Since white carnations were so popular that florists often ran out of their supply on Mother's Day, white became the color worn only if one's mother was deceased. Red carnations then came to symbolize a living mother.

I colored this pretty bouquet of flowers just for you, Mommy.

Mother's Calling

Of all the rights of women,
the greatest is to be a mother.

LIN YUTANG

A mother is the truest friend we have, when trials, heavy and sudden, fall upon us; when adversity takes the place of prosperity; when friends who rejoice with us in our sunshine desert us when troubles thicken around us; still will she cling to us, and endeavor by her kind precepts and counsels to dissipate the clouds of darkness, and cause peace to return to our hearts.

WASHINGTON IRVING

A Mother's Responsibility

God's plan for you was to be a mother—a high calling in our society today. With all of the choices your little one will have to make when she grows older, it is your responsibility to teach her how to make wise decisions. She will learn from your attitudes and follow the path you take.

Your child will pay attention when you. . .

- take a meal to a sick or elderly neighbor.
- smile and offer words of encouragement to a waitress who's having a bad day on the job.
- donate your time to a charitable cause.
- read your Bible, pray, attend church services, and participate in church activities.

Although these are only a few examples of what you may do to encourage your child to reach out to others in kindness and follow God's Word, they bring an important reminder to light: She will learn from your wonderful example.

When you're unsure of the proper response or attitude you should have in order to raise your child God's way, just ask yourself, "What would Jesus do?" and you won't go wrong!

Dear Lord,

Thank You for this calling in my life. Thank You for the gift of my child. Help me to be a good example as I go through my day-to-day tasks and show my little one how important it is to live for You. May my child see Your love through my actions.

Amen.

Mommy, thank you. . .

- for praying for me every day.

- for providing me with good food and clothes, and for meeting all my needs.

- for loving me even when I misbehave and act very UN-lovable.

- for taking me to church so I can learn about Jesus and His love for me.

Thank you for being YOU!

I'm glad you're my mommy
because. . .

_____

_____

_____

_____

_____

_____

_____

Life affords no greater responsibility, no greater privilege,
than the raising of the next generation.

C. EVERETT KOOP

Train a child in the
way he should go,
and when he is old
he will not turn from it.

PROVERBS 22:6

All I am, I owe to my mother.
I attribute all my success in life to the moral, intellectual,
and physical education I received from her.

GEORGE WASHINGTON

The mother's heart
is the child's schoolroom.

HENRY WARD BEECHER

My Mother

Who ran to help me when I fell,
And would some pretty story tell,
Or kiss the place to make it well?
My mother.

JANE AND ANN TAYLOR

May your father and mother be glad; may she who gave you birth rejoice!

PROVERBS 23:25

Nobody knows of the work it makes
To keep the home together.
Nobody knows of the steps it takes.
Nobody knows—but Mother.

AUTHOR UNKNOWN

You make my world brighter,
Mommy!

You know you're a mom when you say things like. . .

- Don't ask me; ask your father.

- Were you raised in a barn? Close the door.

- Get your elbows off the table.

- Who said life was supposed to be fair?

- Because I said so. That's why.

- If I didn't love you so much, I wouldn't punish you. . . .
  I would let you do whatever you wanted.

- You're not leaving the house dressed like that!
  What will other parents think?

- Don't use that tone with me!

- Two wrongs do not make a right.

- Act your age.

- Wipe your feet.

AUTHOR UNKNOWN

There never was a woman like her. She was gentle as a dove and brave as a lioness. . . . The memory of my mother and her teachings were, after all, the only capital I had to start life with, and on that capital I have made my way.

ANDREW JACKSON

A mother is she who can take the place of all others but whose place no one else can take.

CARDINAL MERMILLOD

Here are ways I like spending
time with you, Mommy.

_____

_____

_____

_____

_____

_____

_____

_____

M-O-T-H-E-R

"M" is for the million things she gave me,
"O" means only that she's growing old,
"T" is for the tears she shed to save me,
"H" is for her heart of purest gold;
"E" is for her eyes, with love-light shining,
"R" means right, and right she'll always be,
Put them all together, they spell "MOTHER,"
A word that means the world to me.

HOWARD JOHNSON

To My Mother

For all the times you gently picked me up
When I fell down,
For all the times you tied my shoes
And tucked me into bed,
Or needed something
But put me first instead.
For everything we shared,
The dreams, the laughter,
And the tears,
I love you with a "Special Love"
That deepens every year.

AUTHOR UNKNOWN

Here's a picture I drew
just for you, Mommy.

Here are some things that
I promise to do for you
this week to show you that
I appreciate you, Mommy.

_____

_____

_____

_____

_____

_____

_____

_____

Happy Mother's Day!

You are the World's Best Mommy!

I LOVE YOU!